Living Out the Gospel

By

Pedro Belardo, Jr.

Published by:

McDougal & Associates
18896 Greenwell Springs Road
Greenwell Springs, LA 70739
www.thepublishedword.com

McDougal & Associates is an organization dedicated to spreading the Gospel of the Lord Jesus Christ to as many people as possible in the shortest time possible.

ISBN: 978-1-940461-88-5
eBook 978-1-940461-89-2

Printed in the U.S., the U.K. and Australia
For Worldwide Distribution

Dedication

I dedicate this book:

To my wife, M.L. Wannee Belardo.

To my three children, John Mark, Joy and Jennifer.

To my grandson Prem.

To all my other descendants as yet unborn.

Acknowledgments

My thanks to Harold McDougal. When I first met him and was led to study under him and then join his team of missionaries, I could not have known that now, many years later, he would become my editor and publisher. I am grateful for his patience in making this the best book it could be.

THE BELARDO FAMILY

For to me to live is Christ, and to die is gain.

Philippians 1:21

Contents

Foreword by Joey Tupe

When Pedro Belardo and our other missionary partner, Luciano Cariaga, told me they had to fly to Danang, I urged them not to go. It was April of 1975, and the forces of North Vietnam were already taking over many cities in the south. Most of the other missionaries had already left the country. Only one plane was left, and it was headed to that city near the northern tip of South Vietnam. I was afraid they wouldn't be able to return. But both men insisted they had a strong feeling that the Lord wanted them to go, and so they went.

As a result of that decision, these two men of God were able to persuade the captain of a Philippine Navy boat to allow our Vietnamese pastor friend, Dang Ngoc Cang, and his family of twelve children to leave with them on that boat to Saigon. It was just in time. The North Vietnamese were even then taking the city.

That Vietnamese family eventually arrived, safe and sound, in Akron, Ohio. This is just one example of how my friend and colleague, Pedro, has lived out the Gospel, which he faithfully continues to do even after so many years of serving our Lord.

Peter, Luciano and I all went through the same missionary training back in the early 1970s, and all of us have experienced God's miraculous provision, as so aptly described by Peter in this book. We were often sent to some city or some other nation with a one-way ticket, no monthly support and no contact or assurance of where we would be staying for months or even years. But God was faithful. Inevitably, someone would invite us to stay in their home at no cost, and from there we would launch out, day after day, ministering the Gospel to thousands of people we met everywhere.

This has been our testimony now for the past forty-five years, as we have taken the words of Jesus to His disciples literally:

> *As you go, preach this message: "The Kingdom of Heaven is near ... ." Do not take any gold or silver or copper ... , for the worker is worthy of his keep.* Matthew 10:7-10

Foreword by Joey Tupe

I encourage you to read this powerful true story, and, as you do, let the Lord challenge you. Perhaps you will be the next one to prove the faithfulness of the Lord by going forth by faith, trusting Him alone for your provision.

I also recommend this book as required reading for missions and evangelism classes in Bible schools and seminaries. It will inspire students as they see that even humble Filipinos, who had no guaranteed western financial support, could sometimes have greater results than those who were fully backed by their mission boards. This will inspire students to realize that money is not their problem. Vision, passion and a life of prayer and fasting are the keys to reaching our world for Christ.

Joey Tupe
Quezon City, Philippines

Introduction

This book has been written to proclaim the faithfulness of God. He has been faithful to me since I accepted Him in my youth as my Lord and Savior. Until now, so many years later, His great faithfulness has not changed.

This book also shows the power of God to save and to heal—physically and spiritually. He is still alive today, to heal the sick and the brokenhearted, and to do for us whatever we need Him to do.

Peter Belardo
Bangkok, Thailand

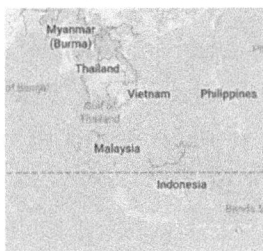

Myanmar
(Burma)

Thailand

Vietnam   Philippines

Malaysia

Indonesia

Chapter 1

My Very Catholic Upbringing

I was born into a very staunch Catholic family and served as a sacristan, or altar boy, throughout my childhood. At a young age, I was accustomed to leading the family in praying the Rosary. My sister Maristela became a teacher in a Catholic school.

For about six months, when I was still in elementary school, I actually lived in the convent and served the sisters, the priest and the church. This was still the time when the Mass and prayers were said in Latin, so until today I remember the Lord's Prayer in Latin. I can still remember running to the tower of the church to ring the bell every evening at 6 p.m., and when I did that, everyone stopped what they were doing and prayed The Angelus. I felt as if I had all power in my hand, being able to make everyone stop walking and start praying just because I rang that bell.

From elementary school through college, I studied in a Catholic school, and I went to church every Sunday. As I got older, however, little by little, I became mired in sin and engaged in various vices: smoking, gambling and hanging out with the wrong crowd. I joined a school gang, and we would often fight with the students of other schools. One time we rode in a jeep and attacked a group of students who were eating at a local restaurant. They ran to the kitchen of the restaurant, and when they came back, they had knives and bolos [1] in their hands. We had only our fists, and so were forced to retreat. One of my good friends was wounded in that melee.

As fellow gang members, we shared our girlfriends with each other. I can say, together with Paul of the Bible, that I was the worst of sinners. But, thank God, in the middle of that darkness, when I was mired in that filth, Jesus found me and pulled me out.

---

1. Similar to a machete. Miriam-Webster defines *bolo* as "a long heavy single-edged knife of Philippine origin used to cut vegetation and as a weapon."

My Very Catholic Upbringing

It happened during the summer of 1970. That summer, when I was twenty-three, the Lord favored me with the eternal life He has promised to every individual who will sincerely seek Him. I had been such a staunch Catholic that I had joined the Legion of Mary and was willing to sacrifice myself to defend Mary from any devilish attack. Then one day I learned that my uncle was coming to our home to visit.

Uncle Caesar had become a born-again Christian a few years before, and he said he wanted to talk to me about God. I got out my many Catechism books so that I could fend off any attack he might make against the Holy Mother. Then I was relaxed, waiting for his coming, confident that I could answer any of his arguments against Catholicism.

When Uncle Caesar finally came, after a short introduction, he asked me a question that dismantled all of my defenses. "If God is without beginning and end, how can Mary, a mere human being, be the mother of God?" I was stunned by the question and found that I had no answer. As a member of the Legion of Mary, I repeated my prayers to the Holy Mother fifty times a day: "Holy Mary, Mother of God, be with us sinners now and at the hour of our death. Amen!" Now, however, I could no longer pray that prayer. Those words suddenly seemed illogical to me.

That night I had a hard time sleeping. My uncle's question kept sounding over and over in my mind. These doubts opened the way for the Holy Spirit to come and convict me of all my pretensions and hypocrisies. My belief that I was a religious man and my holier-than-thou attitude crumbled to pieces. That Sunday I didn't go to the Catholic church as usual, but rather to the small chapel where my uncle was accustomed to going. And that day I gave my life to Jesus.

While I was kneeling at the altar that day, God showed me all of my sins, and I wept and wept and wept some more in repentance. I can't say how long I was there at that altar, but when I opened my eyes, there was no one there except the pastor, who had waited patiently for me. I came out of that church a new man, and the pastor was so happy for me that he gave me a Bible.

From that day on, I could hardly put that book down. There was such a feeling of excitement in every new page I read that I sometimes forgot about the time and forgot to eat. I was totally in love with Jesus.

Chapter 2

My Genesis

In many ways, this was the beginning of my life. Until then, I had breathed but not really lived. I was like the walking dead. Life, from that day forward, became very exciting and very rewarding.

Before I go on, however, let me tell you a little about my earthly family, our town and our church. I was born the third of five children to a fisher family in the town of Cabadbaran in the province of Agusan del Norte on the island of Mindanao. Later, my father, Pedro Sr., got a government job operating a bulldozer, making roads, but when I was born he did what everyone else in our town did—fish. Aside from farming, fishing was the major occupation on our island. Today, new businesses are opening up everywhere across the Philippines, as it has become a major player in the economy of Southeast Asia. There are still plenty of fish, but not everyone is a fisherman or farmer like before.

My oldest brother, Virgilio, died when he was forty. After him came Maristela, our only sister, then me and finally Rodolfo, our baby brother.

When I was young, our town was quite small. Today it has grown so much that it has the designation of a city. [2]

The little church where I got saved was called Agape Church, and it was aptly named because, even though it was small, it was full of God's love. My pastor, Wire Alley Gonzalez, was on fire for God, a man of faith and true service to Christ, and I learned a lot from him. Agape was a Spirit-filled church, and I was soon baptized in the Holy Spirit myself.

Pastor Gonzalez taught us to be soul winners and took us with him as he did evangelism around the town. Drunkards would often mock or otherwise try to disturb our meetings, but Pastor Gonzalez was never afraid and always continued preaching, whatever happened.

When classes started again that fall, I could not be silent about my newfound faith. I was

---

2. In the Philippines, when a town reaches 100,000 in population, it becomes a city and has many legal rights it did not have before.

able to convince one of my teachers to come to our church and be blessed. Some of my classmates responded to my testimony, and others did not. It was all so new to me—and so wonderful!

Of all that happened to me in those days, the greatest was being able to read the Bible for myself. Our family had not owned a Bible as we were growing up. The Bible was only allowed to the priest. Now I could know what God Himself said about any particular topic. I was being freed from empty traditions and brought more and more into the glorious light of the Gospel of Jesus Christ. I loved it and wanted more of it!

Chapter 3

A Golden Opportunity?

Just after I graduated from college, Pastor Gonzalez told me about a campmeeting he had heard about that would be conducted in Surigao City that summer. It sounded wonderful, and fortunately that was not too far for us to be able to attend. A place to sleep and free meals would be provided, so we went.

A group of young American missionaries from the Manila area had secured permission to use the Surigao Stadium, and with them, were some of their Filipino associates. I loved the Gospel these missionaries preached and was impressed with the Filipinos who were with them. The testimonies they gave of serving God in many other places were absolutely wonderful!

It didn't take me long to make the decision to go back with them and enter their missionary training center. But I had to go home first and inform my parents, and that proved to be a most difficult thing.

My decision to serve God created a lot of tension, especially between me and my father. When I asked for his permission to go to the Bible school, he became so angry that he nearly hit me with his fists. He said that he had sacrificed to send me to college, and that sacrifice was not so that I would become involved in some kind of religious activities. His hope had been that I would work and eventually support my parents. I'm not sure his reaction would have been the same if I had chosen to enter the priesthood, but I did have other options.

Because I had graduated with top honors, the college I had attended now offered me a teaching position. They wanted someone to open a high school for them in a nearby town. This offer thrilled my father, and when I declined it, he was doubly angry.

My sister Maristela had also helped me financially with my college studies, and she, too, was very angry that I was "throwing it all away" to attend a Bible school, so angry that she came and took back all the clothes she had bought me.

As I set out for Manila, I had only a small bag of personal belongings. I had one good shirt and one decent pair of pants to my name, so every night I had to wash them out and get them dry and ready to wear again the next day. The director of the Bible school, a young American from West Virginia named Harold McDougal, noticed this and gave me some of his old clothes. The problem was that I was just a mid-sized Filipino, and he was a tall American. Because I had no money to have the clothes altered, I just wore them that way. Some of my friends laughed at me when they saw it. I guess I looked like an Eskimo with those big heavy clothes, but I was happy to wear them until a friend eventually got a burden to alter them to fit me better.

But what had I gotten myself into? This "Bible school" was like none other I had ever heard of before.

Chapter 4

My Introduction to the Work of CTTP

Who were these people I was joining? And why was I so drawn to them? They were all working with a group calling itself Christ to the Philippines. I was to learn that Christ to the Philippines had formed as a result of the vision of the American missionary, Brother Harold, and his Filipino co-workers.

Brother Harold had met a Filipino business-man in a campmeeting in Virginia some years before, and he had then felt a call to join this man in his work in our country. He had thought it would be for a short time only, because another American missionary was scheduled to come out and take his place after sixty days, and he wanted to go on to India. As it turned out, he was in the Philippines for many years — the next seven years to be exact.

In their early years, the McDougals (joined a year later by the Robinson family), had a burden for unreached places. They would organize crusades in outlying areas that had no Spirit-filled church and start one. Country people themselves, the message of these missionaries was very simple, and that appealed to the simple people of our countryside. Most importantly, they asked God to do miracles of healing in each of their meetings, and it was these miracles that convinced many of the validity of their message. Soon churches were established in parts of several provinces, including Rizal, Bulacan, Nueva Ecija, Nueva Vizcaya, Laguna and Maria Aurora and also many areas of the Bicol region—all on the island of Luzon.

Then something changed dramatically in this ministry. Through a series of events known as the Spiritual Fiesta, which were televised in many major cities of our country (including Surigao), the missionaries of Christ to the Philippines, along with their growing number of Filipino associates, began receiving invitations from many of the Catholic institutions, especially those related to priests and nuns, to come and teach on prayer and the infilling of the Holy Spirit.

At the same time, our government opened the public schools to the CTTP teams to go in and teach classroom by classroom, pray with the teachers and students, and place a Gospel of John in the hands of each one. During summer recesses, the CTTP teams would go to the tribal areas of our country, preach and distribute Gospel portions in the languages of the minorities living there. Over a two-year period, more than 1.25 million gospels were placed in this way. Soon the Asian edition of *Time* magazine reported that a thousand priests and nuns and ten thousand Catholic lay people had been filled with the Spirit in the Philippines during this period.

Because of the success of this ministry and its acceptance in high places, there were now weekly live telecasts from the main church in Quezon City and ten radio programs a day over popular stations around the nation, as well as those crusades being conducted in schools, and others on military bases and in selected convents and monasteries. This mission was clearly making a difference in our country, and as I learned of these things, my excitement continued to grow.

When we arrived in the Manila area and I got to the communal living quarters a couple of blocks away from the CTTP mission house, I began to meet many of the other students who were currently preparing themselves through the CTTP Missionary Training Center for a future ministry.

This center was based on an interesting concept: Although Bible teachings were given every day and Bible verses were memorized, more emphasis was placed on prayer and fasting, learning to hear the voice of God and learning to be sensitive to the Holy Spirt's guidance. The students and teachers prayed together every morning for an hour and again in the afternoon. Several evenings a week the students were required to attend services in the church. Often there were special speakers from other countries who would challenge us.

Other subjects that were taught, with the goal in mind of producing missionaries to eventually go out to other nations, were: English Improvement, Geography (especially Asian), and some History of the Asian nations.

Once this classroom training was complete, the students were then formed into teams and sent out to begin what was called their Field Training period. During the coming months, they would work with a more experienced team leader and would do any type of ministry that opened to them. They were expected to preach, teach or testify when called upon, and then pray with those who responded to their message. Their audience might be school students, military recruits, or the members of local churches.

Those students who successfully completed these two training periods were then considered for more serious missionary work in the surrounding nations. In that same two-year period, Filipinos ministered in more than twenty other nations, and that was just the beginning.

Myanmar
(Burma)
Thailand
Vietnam   Philippines
of Bengal
Thailand
Malaysia
Indonesia
Banda S

Chapter 5

Passing the Tests

If I had expected the training to be easy, I was wrong. In the days, weeks and months ahead, I was to go through many trials.

In former years, CTTP had a nice Bible school building they had built in the mountains of Sampaloc, Tanay, Rizal, but a very strong typhoon had damaged that building so severely that it had been abandoned for the time being.

The headquarters of Christ to the Philippines was located at No. 10 11th Avenue, in Cubao, Quezon City. This was also the house where the missionaries lived. Adjacent to the mission house was a church that the missionaries and their associates had built. The entrance to that church was on 12th Avenue. This became our classroom for our Bible school training, and we went there each week-day for prayer and study.

The housing for the rest of us was in a rented building two blocks away on 13th Avenue. It had been erected originally as an old theater building, but it had not been used for many years, so the missionaries rented it, and that was where all the students, as well as any workers who happened to be home at the time, slept and ate.

The building itself was a World War II Quonset hut. For those who may be unfamiliar with this type of building, Dictionary.com states:

> *Quonset hut:* a semicylindrical metal shelter having end walls, usually serving as a barracks, storage shed, or the like, developed for the U.S. military forces from the British Nissen hut at Quonset Naval Base in Rhode Island.

In other words, these were prefab metal buildings used by the military for all kinds of activities, and after the war many were made available to the public through surplus. In fact, Quonset huts are still in use in many parts of the world today. In the U.S., they are especially popular for farm use, I am told.

This particular Quonset hut was very big, but it had been abandoned for many years, and, as noted, had never been used for housing, only as a theater. The Philippine military from nearby Camp Crame sent engineers to help tear out the old balcony risers, to create a level area where beds could be placed for the single ladies and to make more bathroom facilities. So all the ladies stayed upstairs on the balcony, nearer to the metal roof, and it was very hot up there.

The downstairs had few dividers. It had been left as a large open space where people could sit and watch movies. It also had relatively few windows, and because of the metal roof, during the heat of the day, it was nearly unbearable in there.

Quonset huts were never very practical in the Philippines for everyday use without air-conditioning precisely because: (1) Those metal roofs collected heat, and (2) There were few windows to provide ventilation. This particular building had no air-conditioning at all, so those of us who stayed there suffered a lot.

One large room to the side with a sloping floor was filled with homemade bunk beds, and that's where the single men stayed. Other areas of the downstairs were partitioned off to make places for married couples and our cook and her young daughter.

The food for all those who lived in the 13th Street building was prepared en masse and was often not to everyone's liking. At times, it was limited, so that we were forced to fast, whether we wanted to or not.

Another difficult part of that time was that we were being taught to "live by faith," which meant that we had to trust God completely to supply everything we needed, even our basic daily needs. That was very difficult for those who had no source of income. It was a trying time for all of us, to say the least. We had to learn to trust God for absolutely everything.

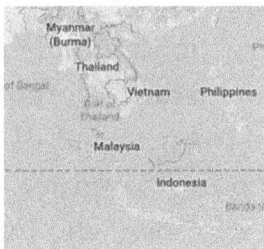

Chapter 6

The Faithfulness of God

Often, during the early weeks of out training, I just didn't have the personal items I needed and no money to buy them. Little by little, I learned to trust God for the smallest things, and He showed Himself faithful to provide for me just at the right time.

One evening, for instance, I had only a few pesos in my pocket and was planning to buy some bread right after the service ended. But then, while the service was going on, God spoke to me and told me to place every centavo I had in the offering plate. I really struggled with that because I had other personal needs besides the bread I had been looking forward to. The more I argued with God, the more uneasy I became as the offering plate came ever nearer. In the end, the conviction of the Spirit was so great that I gave everything I had in my pocket that night.

After the service had ended, I continued praying for a while. I needed God to miraculously provide all of my needs, and yet He had asked me to give the little I had. That didn't seem to make sense. While I was still praying, I felt someone reaching into my shirt pocket. With excitement, I opened one eye and saw there a folded envelope. I immediately left the church and opened the envelop. To my amazement, there was a large amount of money in it, more than enough for my current needs. In fact, that blessing lasted me for weeks to come. God had proved to me that He was trustworthy, and in this way, He taught me to trust Him for everything I needed.

One big thing I gained from that training was a much deeper compassion for the lost. One day, during one of our crusades in Bulacan Province, Brother Luciano Cariaga and I were distributing tracts to anyone we could see and inviting them to come to the meetings. We passed by a group of people who were drinking wine and decided to give them tracts too. The leader of the group thanked us and then offered us a glass of wine as a token of friendship. When we told him that we didn't drink, he took it as a personal insult and was so angry that he smashed the wine bottle in his hand over Brother Luciano's mouth and then jabbed the broken end of the glass into my forehead. The other members of our team took us to a local clinic, and a nurse there stitched us up.

When we got back to the crusade site, Luciano and I were both covered with blood, but we were praising God that He had saved us from something that could have been much worse. I still carry the scars of that event today, and it is a constant reminder to me never to lose the vision of Jesus and His love for the lost.

As a happy footnote to my training period, I prayed every day for my family. This led not only to me being reconciled with my sister and father, but also to their salvation. God is so good!

Chapter 7

A Vision for Souls

I have since attended other training programs, but it was at CTTP where I gained a vision for souls and received a call from God to preach the Gospel to the perishing. It happened one night during our training.

I can't remember exactly who was preaching that night, but what I do remember is that I saw a vision of people falling off of a cliff one by one. Realizing that there was no one to warn them, I cried out to God, "Lord, use me to warn people about Hell."

I was convinced and still am today that Hell is just as real as Heaven is. To my way of thinking, Hell is in the center of the earth. The core of the earth, we are told, is solid rock, but around that rock is burning lava, which burns day and night. That is exactly the way the Bible describes Hell, as a lake of fire that burns continually. From that moment on, I was consumed by a burden for lost souls. That burden , which continues to burn within me until now, was my motivation to reach out wherever I could with the Gospel.

Chapter 8

Going Out in Faith

During our particular field training, we were sent out two by two with a one-way ticket to an assigned province. I was glad to have Brother Luciano as my partner. He was from the Bicol Region. We were first sent to Iloilo, a small central province of the Philippines. We arrived in Iloilo City at night and were startled to see people in tribal costumes dancing and shouting in the streets. Not sure what exactly was going on, we decided to go to the nearest police station and ask if we could spend the night there. The officer in charge allowed us to sleep on some vacant tables.

We learned from the officers that what we had seen was not real tribal people; it was Ati Atihan, a yearly festival held in the city. The local people had just dressed up like tribesmen.

The next day, because we had no contacts, we decided to board a local jeepney, [3] not knowing exactly where we should go. As we rode along in that jeep, we kept praying that God would guide us. Eventually one of the passengers on the jeep asked us who we were and where we were going. We told him, and he immediately broke into a big smile. He was a pastor, and he invited us to stay with him in his church for as long as we were in the area.

From that location, we were able to reach nearly all the towns of that island and even to go to the mountainous areas. Sometimes this required many hours of walking on our part because some of the towns were not accessible by road. As we walked, we carried boxes filled with Gospels of John on our shoulders. When we reached our destination and saw hundreds of eager students, we forgot about our tiredness. During those days, we preached in every high school and college in the area, and when we saw hundreds of students raising their hands

3. Wikipedia says of the jeepney: "sometimes called simply jeeps (Filipino: dyip), they are buses and the most popular means of public transportation ubiquitous in the Philippines. They are known for their crowded vis-à-vis seating and kitsch decorations, which have become a widespread symbol of Philippine culture and art. https://en.wikipedia.org/wiki/Jeepney

Going Out in Faith

to accept the Lord as their personal Savior, we knew it was worth every sacrifice. Some of those towns were hearing the Gospel for the very first time, and only eternity will tell the full story.

Going Out in Faith

to accept the Lord as their personal Savior, we knew it was worth every sacrifice. Some of those towns were hearing the Gospel for the very first time, and only eternity will tell the full story.

41

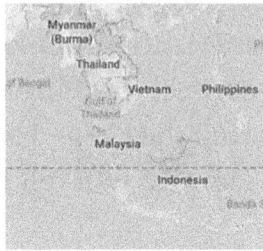

Chapter 9

Singapore, Malaysia and Indonesia

In 1972, after our field training period was complete, we were sent out of the country, to Singapore. As it turned out, our trip would also take us to Malaysia and Indonesia. It was in Indonesia that we were to see the mightiest move of God in our ministry, but it was all good. As always, we were sent out to Singapore with a one-way ticket and not much money in our pockets. In this case, we had just US $120.00, not much when you are traveling abroad.

While we were ministering in some churches in Singapore, the ship known as *Logos* arrived. The *Logos* is a floating Christian bookstore. The next destination for the ship was Indonesia. Since God had spoken to us to go to Indonesia, we asked the captain of the ship if we might be able to travel on the ship with them to Indonesia. He was willing to accommodate us, and in this way, God answered our prayers and sent us to another nation.

Once inside Indonesia, we travelled from Jakarta to Bandung, then to Surabaya and on to Menado in the Celebes Islands. While we were on the bus travelling to Bandung, someone stole my wallet, together with my passport. Now what could I do? My money was gone, and worse, I had no papers. I fasted and prayed for three days, and God blessed us so much financially that I was able to get a new passport through the Philippine Embassy.

While we were in Surabaya, which is located at the eastern end of the island of Java, a pastor from Menado heard us preaching and invited us to be the revival-meeting speakers in his church. We were excited to go with him. When we arrived at the church in Menado, however, the elders of the church were not happy to see how young we were. They reprimanded the pastor for bringing such young preachers in for a big and important revival meeting. The meeting had been scheduled to last a week, but after they saw us, it was cut to three days. Then, the first night of the revival meetings, God showed again that it's not by might, nor by power, but by His Spirit that things get done.

That night I was preaching as I normally did, but to my amazement, before I had finished preaching and before the altar call could be given, the Holy Spirit moved with great conviction upon the people, and they began to come spontaneously to the altar, weeping and repenting of their sins. I was encouraged by this and wanted to preach some more, but I could not do it because the only available interpreter was on the floor with the rest of the people, weeping and worshiping the Lord. When the elders saw how God had moved, they quickly extended the revival meetings back to the originally scheduled week.

Every night that week God moved in such a way that the one-week revival meeting continued in other churches. All in all, the meetings lasted for a full month, and God moved every single night in that same unusual way.

This created a problem for me. I was a young preacher, and I soon ran out of things I knew to preach on. All I could do was pray, and then

Singapore, Malaysia and Indonesia

I stood before the pulpit, having only a few verses in mind and not really knowing how to expound on them. But when I opened my mouth, words just keep on flooding into my mind, and I continued speaking them until I was finished. Sometimes these impromptu sermons lasted a full hour. Some pastors testified that they had not witnessed such miraculous things since the famous American evangelist, T.L. Osborne, had visited Indonesia years before.

We left that place with many blessings, and nearly all of the churches sent groups with us to the airport to send us off. There was a long line of cars, as if some important government official was leaving. God is so good!

This should be an encouragement to every young person. No matter how young you are, if you give your life fully to God without reservation, He will use you to shake cities, provinces and even whole countries by His power.

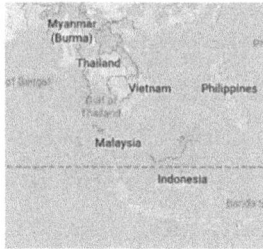

Chapter 10

Vietnam

In 1975, God gave us a new assignment. This time it was Vietnam. As usual, we went there with only a one-way ticket. The problem was that the Vietnam War was still in full swing.

We went straight to the remote northern South Vietnamese town of Tam Ky, where two of our ministry companions from the Philippines, Joey Tupe and Celso Sumido, were waiting to receive us. We were to be their replacements.

Tam Ky was an amazing place. One day the chief of the town invited us to ride with him in a military helicopter to survey the entire area.

It was in this city of Tam Ky that we first met Paul Ai. The Apostle Paul, as he is now widely known, was very young then, and he was also a very new Christian. He had accepted Jesus though Joey and Celso. After they left, he lived with us in a small house there. When we ate, Paul ate. When we slept, Paul slept. And when we prayed, Paul had to pray too. By living so closely with us, Paul received everything that we had. All of our craziness for Jesus was transferred to him.

Discipleship is a lot more than just teaching from a book; it is life experienced with your disciples. That's what Jesus did. He ate and lived with His disciples. No wonder they received the same enthusiasm as He had. Mere teaching is not enough to develop real disciples. If you want to disciple someone, do it like Jesus did.

With Paul Ai as our interpreter, we preached the Gospel with great enthusiasm to all the villages around that town. We received such joy from this that the idea came to us that the best way to die would be while preaching in these dangerous places. When people warned us not to go to a certain village because it was full of Vietcong guerillas, Luciano and I just looked at each other and decided that this was the place we *should* go. Because of this idea we had (that many, I'm sure, would have considered rather weird), many remote and dangerous villages had the Gospel preached to them, and the result was that many hundreds accepted the Lord as their personal Savior.

Often, while we were preaching in Vietnam, we could hear gunfire nearby. We never stopped because of it. We just kept on preaching, and our interpreter had no choice but to continue interpreting. The North Vietnamese Army was advancing, and province after province was falling into their hands … until they were nearing Da Nang.

Da Nang was a beautiful city in the northern part of South Vietnam, and Tam Ky was under it governmentally. When the missionaries of the Assemblies of God (with whom we were working there) realized that nothing could now stop the Communist advance, they decided to resettle the Christians of Tam Ky to another village just eighty kilometers outside of Saigon. We felt like we were like Moses and Aaron, as, along with Pastor Tho of the Assembly of God, we led the Christians in a long line of buses toward Saigon and ended at a new village named Long Thanh.

Chapter 11

Living in the
Resettlement Village

We stayed with the three hundred and fifty Vietnamese Christians in their resettlement village and continued to minister to them. In the physical, they were very poor, having been able to bring very little with them, but in their hearts and spirits, they were indeed rich. Each family took their turn at feeding us, and we were happy living in that village together with our brethren.

The houses in the resettlement village were small wooden structures, and none of them had a toilet. Our toilet was in the tall bushes that stood some meters behind the houses. We had to be careful to find a new spot each time, so we covered a lot of territory.

Then one day, without warning, the South Vietnamese Army set fire to all of that brush area. They had been afraid it would become a hiding place for the Communists to come and attack the village. To our amazement and bewilderment, we suddenly heard landmines exploding as the area burned. No one had known that the area we had been using as our outdoor toilet had actually been a minefield. I firmly believe that every day, as we went into that area, God had been guiding our footstep, just as He promised He would:

> *The steps of a good man are ordered by the LORD: and he delighteth in his way. Though he fall, he shall not be utterly cast down: for the LORD upholdeth him with his hand.*
>   Psalm 37:23-24

Through these experiences, God showed us clearly that He is truly our Shield in times of trouble.

Chapter 12

Safe in the Arms of Jesus

Every day in Long Thanh was just like Christmas because we were situated between the camp of the South Vietnamese Army and the camp of the Vietcong. When the Army launched a missile against the Vietcong, it passed by our village. And when the Vietcong responded, their missile passed our village going the other way.

One night we were sleeping very soundly after preaching and ministering to the people. Just after midnight we heard a long whistle, the sound of an incoming missile. It fell about a hundred meters from the house, and it jolted us. Luciano was an ex-Army man, and he ran out of the house, trying to seek cover in a big hole we had dug to bury our trash. But before Luciano could reach that hole, another missile came in, and he ran back to the house.

The two of us knelt down, heavy with the thought that this might well be our end, but when we began to praise the Lord, all of our worries were suddenly gone. We told God that if a third missile came and fell right on our heads, we were ready. The third missile came, and it smashed right through our simple wooden walls. Luciano had been sleeping on a mosquito net. It was now gone with all of the mosquitoes in it. It was truly a miracle that not even one bit of shrapnel touched either of us. We were completely safe in the arms of God! Praise the wonderful name of Jesus!

Chapter 13

The Church of Vietnam Has Its Pentecost

The Vietnamese believers built a big church in the center of the village that could accommodate more than five hundred people, and it was now full every time we met. The roof of the building was made of grass, there were no sides, the seating was just some small logs, and our floor was just dirt. But what happened inside that primitive building was glorious.

The majority of the people were all new Christians, not yet baptized in the Holy Spirit, so we fasted and prayed for three days that they would receive this experience. They needed the Holy Spirit so that they would have strength and power to maintain their relationship with Jesus, even if they came under the rule of the advancing Communists.

Thank God, He always answers prayer. One night, while a young Bible student was preaching, the Holy Spirit fell mightily on the crowd. It came as a great wave. It first hit the back row, and those sitting there were all jolted as if they had been hit with lightning. Simultaneously they all fell to the ground and began speaking in tongues. Then the wave moved forward and caught everyone in its path. And it wasn't just one wave. Wave after wave moved from the back to the front row.

We usually placed the children on the ground in front so that they could be closely watched and none of them would be running around during the service. After the wave of God's presence hit the front row, it continued forward until it hit the children, and they also began weeping and speaking in tongues.

This move of God started in the early hours of the evening and it lasted until the next morning. There was no stopping it, and we didn't try. We just stood aside and let the Holy Spirit do His work. From that day on, we didn't worry about the Church in Vietnam. It had a strong foundation, and we were sure that nothing could stop it, not even Communism. From then until the end, the Christians all met to pray with us every morning at 5:00 a.m. in the church.

One of those who witnessed and experienced that great move was Paul Ai. From that time on, he truly became the Apostle Paul of Vietnam and went on to do mighty things for God.

Chapter 14

Going to Da Nang?

A few days after that revival, while we were praying, Luciano told me that he felt like God was telling him to go back to Da Nang. I laughed, thinking that he was just making a joke. We had heard on the radio that Da Nang was already surrounded and would fall to the Communists at any moment.

When I saw that Luciano was dead serious, I challenged him. If it was God who spoke that to him, then I would open my Bible randomly, close my eyes and place my finger on one verse, and if it contained the word *go*, I would actually go with him. I didn't really believe in being led in that way, but I did it just to satisfy him. To my utter amazement, my finger landed on a verse that contained the word *go*. I was speechless. I had given my word, and I couldn't go back on it.

Going to Da Nang?

On the way to the airport, I was still hoping that something would prevent us from going. Surely there were no more planes going to Da Nang! But, when we arrived at the airport, we learned that there was one more American plane going to Da Nang. It was a big one and it was being sent to evacuate the last of the Americans from that beleaguered city. We boarded that plane as if we were the owners. We were the only passengers, and it carried us for free.

We were excited to get to Da Nang and see our brothers who were still there. But, instead of them being glad to see us, they scolded us and told us to get back to the airport immediately and board the same plane and get out. Everything in the city was very chaotic. Everybody was running here and there, not knowing how to escape from the Communists who were tightening their stranglehold on the city. It was no place for us.

Confused, we obeyed, but when we got back to the airport, it was even more chaotic, and when we inquired about the plane that had brought us there, we were told that it was already filled. We went back into the city, more confused and not knowing what to do next. I went straight to the banks of the beautiful Da Nang River and began to pray. I also did some complaining. Had God told us to come back here just to be stranded? That didn't make sense. While I was walking along the river praying, I noticed a small ship with a Philippine flag on it.

When I talked to the men in charge of it, they told me that their purpose was to take all Filipinos and their dependents out of the city, as ordered by then President Ferdinand Marcos. Right then and there, God answered my question about why He had sent us back to Da Nang. We were being rescued.

I was sure that the Lord wanted us to take with us all of our Vietnamese brothers (who had no other way of escaping). We were told that, as Filipinos, we would be given the privilege to board the ship first, but that, yes, we could go together with our Vietnamese brothers.

The Filipino vessel was a transport ship, used to transport tanks and other military vehicles, and it could accommodate thousands of people. When we boarded the ship, there were still thousands upon thousands of Vietnamese standing by, hoping that they could also board and get out of the city.

Since it was such a big cargo ship, there was still enough room to accommodate another one or even two thousand people. When the door was opened for the Vietnamese people to board, however, that huge crowd surged forward. Then, when the limit of capacity had been reached, the door was suddenly forced shut, and the ship slowly left the pier.

Believe me that was a terrible sight! Desperate cries could be heard throughout the crowd. Some fathers and mothers had been able to board, and their children had been left behind. Some children had been able to board, and their parents were left behind. Many jumped off of the ship and swam back to shore, not willing to be separated from their loved ones. But many children were not able to jump or to swim, and they were separated from their parents. I have no way of knowing if they were ever reunited with their loved ones. No one should ever have to suffer such deep agony!

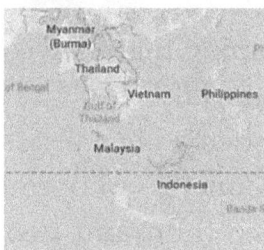

Chapter 15

Saying Goodbye to Vietnam

When we arrived in Saigon, we brought the Vietnamese brothers to the resettlement village, and many of them were happily reunited with their families. We had loved our time there with the Vietnamese. They had taken such good care of us physically, and it had been our privilege to care for them spiritually. We had loved that simple wooden church with its hundreds of congregants. Now, however, we received an official notice from the Philippine Embassy that we would have to go back home as it seemed imminent that the Communists would soon take over the whole of South Vietnam.

We left Vietnam with a heavy heart, not happy to leave our Vietnamese brothers, and we would not have done it had it not been ordered. We had to obey, in spite of the protests of our dear Brother Paul Ai. He reminded us of one of my favorite sermon topics:

For to me to live is Christ, and to die is gain. Philippians 1:21

But we had to keep in mind another scripture, one that told us to obey those in authority. In days to come, we learned that Paul Ai was in and out of prison, but that he was continuing to preach the Gospel and establish churches. When he was free, he preached and established churches, and when the authorities caught him, he preached and established churches in the prisons. No one could stop him because he was so crazy for Jesus.

Back in the Philippines now, Luciano and I helped with the teaching in the Christ to the Philippines Bible School, and we were happy there. I was especially happy because I had met a beautiful lady that I hoped one day to make my wife. Luciano had also met someone, and they began to plan their future together.

We soon learned that the Communists had successfully invaded all of South Vietnam and

Laos, and the talk of the moment was that the next country to fall would be Thailand. It was the Domino Theory that, until then, had proven to be all too true. When Luciano and I heard that, immediately God gave us a burden to go to Thailand and work with the refugees and also train the Thai Christians before the Communists could come there.

It was 1976, and we were on our way to Thailand. Alas! The young lady I had hoped to make my wife was determined to go to the Middle East instead. My heart sank even as I knew that I was doing God's will and starting a new and exciting chapter of my life.

Chapter 16

Hello, Thailand!

As before, we were going to another country with a one-way ticket and an allowance large enough only to insure our survival for a few days, and we had absolutely no contacts in Thailand. When we arrived in Bangkok, we had no choice but to stay in a cheap hotel—the local YMCA.

After one week, our money was nearly gone, and we had to get out of the hotel, not knowing where we should go. The two of us walked along Sathorn Road, dragging our bags with us. We tried to read the signs, but the Thai writing just looked like worms to us. We were hungry and tired and tried to sleep in a bus stop. But there was just no way to sleep because the Thai mosquitoes were very big and voracious.

The next morning we went back to the YMCA and asked if the staff there knew of any Filipino pastors in the city. We looked so tired that they pitied us and tried their best to scan the phone directory for Filipinos. Eventually they said they had found one. We were excited about it and asked them to please write down the address in Thai.

We gave the address to the driver of a *tuk-tuk* (a three-wheeled taxi), and when he read it, a big smile came over his face and he said, "Okay! Okay!" We went around and around for the next hour or so, but the driver couldn't seem to find the address. He eventually stopped the *tuk-tuk* and turned to look at us. He tried to mutter something, but we couldn't understand, so we just looked at him with a big question mark.

I think the man wanted us to get out of the *tuk-tuk*, but we had to stay put because we had no money to pay him. He started the *tuk-tuk* again and went around and around again, but still he could not find the address on the paper.

This time, he stopped and looked at us with big red eyes. We decided we had better get out or the man might give us a good Thai kick, like we had seen on TV. We told him to wait, and we went to inquire at the house he had stopped in front of. We were pleasantly surprised to find that the owners of the house were also Filipinos, though not the pastor we were looking for. They were very kind to us, welcoming us to stay with them. They also volunteered to pay the *tuk-tuk* for us. Hallelujah! God is always on time!

After spending a little more time with the owners, what had happened made more sense to us. They were an older couple and were longing for their children who were scattered around the world. Of the hundreds of houses that we passed by, God had led us to the right house and the right family for us to stay with. They took care of us just like their own children, and we were eating hotel food every day because the wife was catering food for a local hotel.

While we stayed with this couple, we contacted different churches, and they invited us to preach and sing for them. In the process, God blessed us abundantly with material and spiritual blessings.

We met a beautiful lady who was a broadcaster with a Christian television program, and she invited us to sing on the show. This was a great help in making our presence felt in the country.

This lady was Rev. Buakhab Ronghanan, and she is still active in the ministry today.

One day we went to a Christian bookstore in Silom Road, and while there, we heard someone playing Christian music on the third floor of the building. We went up and met a young man named Anuchit Rotsansern, and he became our interpreter and brought us to many different places in Bangkok. Also, the owner of the building, the late Adjarn Preeda Chantrakul, pitied us and let us stay on the third floor of the building. I had been feeling that we needed to transfer from the Filipino house because we didn't want to wear out our welcome.

On the third floor, where we were now living, there was also a church. The young people of that church loved us intensely and took very good care of us. We became de-facto pastors of the church because it was the owner of the building who had been pastoring at the same time, but he was already quite elderly.

As Anuchit brought us to different places to meet Christians and visit and minister in their churches, one of the astounding things that happened was the baptism of the Holy Spirit falling on the young people in a Presbyterian church.

From there, it spread to other churches. Many of the Thai churches were so traditional that they refused the baptism of the Holy Spirit, but, praise God, when the fire of God begins to burn, nothing can stop it. It will surely spread like wildfire, and that is what happened. This spontaneous outpouring spread to many other churches.

Because of this move of God, the invitations coming in from other churches were more than we could handle, so we asked for reinforcements from the Philippines. God answered our prayers and sent reinforcements from Christ to the Philippines: Revs. Sonny Lagardo and Mario Taculod.

Before long, Brother Sonny encouraged us to establish a legal covering under the Evangelical Fellowship of Thailand, and he suggested me as the first Director. At first, I didn't like this idea. I told Brother Sonny that our leaders had sent us to Thailand, not to establish an organization, but just to preach the Gospel. However, the majority won. Thank God for Brother Sonny, the youngest in the group. It is because of him that Christ to Thailand Mission came into existence.

After eight months, Luciano and I went back to the Philippines, leaving our reinforcements to continue the work in Thailand.

Chapter 17

What Now?

Back in the Philippines, we returned to teaching in the Bible school and also engaged in evangelism and revival meetings in different churches and other places. After about a year, we had an urgent message from the young people in the church in Thailand. They had been led to gather enough money for our fare going back to Thailand. We prayed about it and saw it as God's will for us to go back. It was 1978, and we were on our way to Thailand again.

We had a Filipino friend in Hong Kong, so we passed through there on our way to Bangkok. While in Hong Kong, we preached in several local churches. In the process, we met an evangelist named Wayne Crooke. Wayne was on his third day of fasting and was asking God for a contact to go to Thailand. He was very happy to see us and saw our meeting as a direct answer from God to his prayer.

Soon after we had arrived back in Thailand, we felt led to conduct a youth camp and invited young people from many different churches in Bangkok. More or less two hundred young people attended. One of those attendees was a beautiful young lady known as Mom Luang [her royal title] Wannie Chayangkul. After I had ministered in one of the services, she came to tell me what a blessing it had been to her. It was the beginning of a deep friendship that ultimately blossomed into an even more exciting relationship.

This lady carried a royal title that I did not fully understand in the beginning. My Thai friends could hardly believe my luck. I was just an ordinary guy, living by faith, and this woman was so beautiful and so sweet, and she was carrying a royal title. It had to be God who brought us together. It would not have been possible otherwise because we were so different from each other, with very different family backgrounds. She was a teacher in one of the high schools in Bangkok.

After only a few months of dating, Wannie and I decided to get married, and the first hurdle I had to pass was how to tell her parents. I decided to bring along two Christian brothers I considered to be my parents away from home. They were both businessmen, so I was confident that, with them acting as my parents, there would be no problem. I was wrong.

When we met Wannie's parents, all they could say was "No! No! and No!" Their main reason was that they were pure Thai, and they didn't want their daughter to marry a foreigner. My two daddies and I could not say anything more as they flatly rejected us.

However, my fiancée, their daughter, was able to talk to them, and she talked for quite some time. Her parents seemed to be dumbfounded by what she was saying and could not say anything. I couldn't understand much Thai yet, but it seemed to me that her central argument was that she was of age already, and so she had the right to decide for herself who she would marry. In the end, her parents gave their consent, and we tied the knot on June 16, 1979.

I didn't have much money at the time, but all of my Thai friends contributed toward the wedding expenses. Anuchit gave the bulk of the money. A Thai lady volunteered to make the cake for us, and it was beautiful three-tiered cake. We were married in Wannie's church with her pastor officiating. Thank God for the success of the wedding. It was He who prepared everything. It was a good start to our marriage.

Chapter 18

Back to Work

After the wedding, we took a week's honeymoon in Pattaya, a famous tourist attraction on the Thai coast. Then, it was back to work again for both of us. We continued having revival meetings in different churches and also open-air meetings.

By now, we badly needed a car for the ministry, and praise God, the late Brother Wayne Crooke sent us a van. We called that van Lazarus because he had resurrected it. It was already old, but it still had a lot of good use in it. We used that van for crusades in many different provinces.

We travelled from province to province, conducting healing crusades, and because of the miracles God did, thousands came to the Lord. Our advertising was simple. We printed leaflets with the wording:

Miracles! Miracles!
The lame can walk,
and blind eyes can see
by the power of God!

In one of the crusades in the north, God moved so mightily that we might call it an "historic" crusade. It was the first time something like this had happened in Thailand. The crowd swelled after one notable miracle. A completely paralyzed woman stood and walked after we prayed for her. She was only skin and bones and could not even move when she was brought for prayer.

I looked at her and then, taking her by the hand, I said, "In the name of Jesus, stand up and walk." I offered to help her, and slowly she stood up.

Next, I commanded her to walk, and she walked slowly. Then I told her to run, and she began excitedly running across the stage.

I assured the crowd that we were not the healers. It was Jesus who had healed this woman. The crowd roared in unison, "God is great!" and "Thank You, Jesus!"

Another notable miracle was the stopping of the rain. One night, just as the meeting was about to start, it started to rain. We prayed for the rain to stop and, praise God, it did. We looked up, and it seemed that there was a hole looking up to Heaven. Above us we could see the stars, but all around us, the sky was very dark. The people who were still coming were drenched with the rain, but the grounds where we were conducting the meeting were dry.

After that miracle we could see big trucks filled with people coming to the crusade. Twenty thousand people filled the school ground every night. It was a blessing to see many pastors kneeling down and saying, "Lord, I believe! Lord, I believe!" They belonged to traditional churches that didn't believe in miracles, healing and the baptism of the Holy Spirit. Before this time, there had been very few Thai people who had heard about the Holy Spirit, but after that pastors came to us to be prayed for to receive this glorious infilling.

Something, however, was seriously lacking. After a few months, when we visited that place again, most of the new believers were nowhere to be found. They had gone back to their former religion. We asked many questions, searched our own hearts and prayed to see if we could learn what had gone wrong. We found that we were to blame. We had not followed up with these new believers, so they didn't know what to do with their new-found faith, and the result was that they slid back. The need to train more Christians kept burning in our hearts, and we prayed that God would guide us and provide the needs for establishing a training center in Thailand.

Chapter 19

The Training Center in Khonkaen

With the help of Open Doors of Manila, we established a short-term training center in Khonkaen with Brother Rudy Manalac. Khonkaen was chosen because one the leaders saw the northeast part of Thailand burning. This was confirmed again with a vision of a spotlight focused on Khonkaen.

The idea of moving to Khonkaen, however, presented a struggle for me. When I told my wife about it, she said she didn't want to go there. Her parents also scolded me. Why did I have to take my wife to such a remote place? They didn't want us to go to Khonkaen because the northeast part of Thailand was known as the driest part of the country. Besides that, my wife was teaching in the school, and she didn't want to resign from her position.

My life to that point had been to hear from God and then obey Him, no matter who or what opposed it, and God had honored that stand. I was fully convinced now that it was the will of God for me to go to Khonkaen to establish the training center, so I told my wife that I had to go, and she relented and went with me.

We rented a house in Khonkaen, and then we began visiting the churches in the area to tell them about our plan for a short-term training center. The pastors we talked to laughed at this idea. "What can a three-month training do?" They had been to three-year Bible schools, and some of the students still backslid after studying the Bible that long. We were not discouraged by this response and just focused on those who liked the idea. We had about thirty students for our first training in that rented house.

We accepted students from all walks of life, even new Christians and even non-Christians. A few who came were still drinking. Their pastors brought them to us, hoping that they would be changed by our program. We accepted all of them because Jesus' disciples had also come from all walks of life.

Although we accepted all comers, however, we began by emphasizing that we would expect strict obedience to our rules, and one of those rules was that we always prayed at 5 am each morning. Once a month we would be having all-night prayer with fasting. Anyone who was not willing to follow the rules of the course would be dismissed immediately.

I was willing to take a gamble on these students because I truly and sincerely believed in the power of prayer to change them. And, sure enough, through our times of prayer, the lives of those student were completely changed. I saw one of the young men who had come to the training drunk weep and weep during one of the overnight prayer meetings. After that encounter, he was completely changed and became an ardent disciple of Jesus.

After the classroom training was finished, the students were required to undergo field training for another eight months before they could graduate. We held the training every other quarter, using the thee months between to visit the trainees wherever they were, whether in the mountains or in the valleys, observing their work and encouraging them any way we could.

Sometimes we had to hike for an entire day, passing many mountain ranges, to reach a student. This was quite tiring, but when we finally saw each other and had the joy of reuniting, all tiredness was gone. We were like a father and son being reunited after not having seen each other for quite some time. Many of these students got tired and discouraged in their service to God, and it was always an encouragement to them for us pay them a visit.

After their training was finished, we sent the students back to their churches, and the pastors who had sent them could not believe what they now saw. The lifeless people they had sent were now on fire and ready to serve the Lord. After that first time, we never again had a problem recruiting students for our training program. Many came.

Chapter 20

Continuing the Vision

After about a year, the other Filipinos in the organization decided that it was time for them to go back to the Philippines. We didn't have that same feeling, and so we decided to stay and stand on our own. In the beginning, this was completely by faith. We had a few supporters, but their meagre support just did not meet our needs. At times we had to declare forced fasting, if there was not enough rice for us all.

This was a difficult time, but the faith of the students was strengthened through these experiences. Later, when they went back to their churches, they were more prepared to face difficulties when serving the Lord.

After a while, I felt led to establish a church right there in the training center. It was known as Namprathai Church, Khonkaen. This proved to be a good move because it gave the students experience in a real church setting and better prepared them to return to their own churches.

I was also led to establish a committee of pastors from different churches to help us. God did a wonderful miracle for us. I met a Singaporean missionary, the late Rev. Gerald Khoo of the Anglican Church, and through him, the local Anglican church became our best supporter. Each month I prepared a financial report to present to the committee to show the pastors what we were receiving, where it was coming from and how it was being spent.

My original principle had been that the trainees should only serve the Lord and not engage in secular work. They should know how to trust God, even if they had a desire to plant a church. This principle changed when a group of trainees went back to Bangkok and soon found work in various factories. In those factories they opened cell groups for the other workers, and, praise the Lord, many factory workers were saved in this way. From that time on, I was no longer against any students finding work in the place they lived and ministered.

In fact, this now became part of my strategy. I began looking for some work support for any student wanting to establish a church. And when any student told me that he had a burden to establish a church in a certain place, I encouraged him to look for some work in that place and then establish his church by beginning with a cell group in his newfound place of work.

To date, we have trained more than two thousand students. Admittedly, some of them backslid, but many others continue to serve the Lord and to plant churches wherever they go.

Not all of these worked with our church organization. If they found an organization that would serve as an umbrella of legal protection for them, that was fine with me. I did not consider it to be important what organization they belonged to or what the name of their church was. What was important was that a church was being planted for the glory of the Lord Jesus.

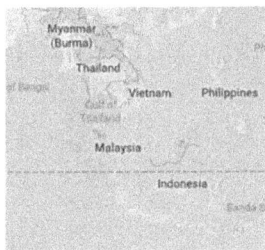

Chapter 21

The Church in Bangkok

While we were doing the worker training in Khonkaen, I also felt a burden to establish a church in Bangkok. I felt that our organization, Christ to Thailand Mission, should have a very large church in the capital city. This was to be a challenge for me. From Monday to Friday I managed the training center, and then I went to Bangkok for Saturday and Sunday. This was very tiring, but, thank God, our labor was not in vain in the Lord. Namprathai Church, Bangkok soon began to take shape.

We established the church using the car tent of Brother Anuchit Rotsansern, and he was the main supporter of the effort. Within three months, God had blessed us, and we already had seventy members. On Saturdays, I visited homes, doing personal evangelism, along with the other leaders of the church. In time, Anuchit used his own funds to build a church building that could accommodate about a hundred worshipers.

During our Sunday worship services, the Holy Spirit would move on the people, and there would be times of weeping and times of dancing. Once, as I was serving Communion to the people, the Holy Spirit fell on all of us so that we were all weeping before the Lord.

I pastored the church for about a year, and then I handed the baton to Pastor Adjarn Anuchit Rotsansern. Until now, the church is growing under the leadership of Pastor Lorna Avenido, with other Filipino pastors serving under her.

Chapter 22

Escaping Every Danger

Over the years, we travelled almost all of the provinces in Thailand, from the north to the south. Sometimes this travel was quite dangerous, but God kept us safe at all times. On one occasion, I was alone, driving from the north back home to Khonkaen. When I reached the mountain ranges that I had to pass, it was already dark. It was so cold up there in the mountains that fog had formed in many places, and I could hardly see the road. I drove very slowly and cautiously.

Then I suddenly heard a loud voice saying, "Stop!" I immediately stepped on the brakes. When the dense fog had lifted a little, I saw that I had been about to go over a steep cliff. Thank God that when we are serving Him, His hands and His angels will always be there to keep us safe.

As the psalmist sang:

Yea, though I walk through the valley of the shadow of death, I will fear no evil: for thou art with me; thy rod and thy staff they comfort me. Psalm 23:4

The Great Shepherd, using His rod and His staff, is always there to keep us safe from harm.

Over the years, I have been near death many times as I served the Lord, but in every one of those times God has proven that His promises are true and that His faithfulness is from everlasting to everlasting. He is the God of the Universe, and He is in control of every situation of our lives.

Chapter 23

Moving On?

After more than ten years of running the training center myself, I gave the responsibility to my colleagues in the Christ to Thailand Mission, and since then they have carried on that wonderful work. Also, after those first years of the organization under my leadership, the baton was passed to Rev. Sonny Lagardo, a fellow Filipino, and he has taken the organization forward ever since.

Although I was considered to be quite old at that point (I am sixty-nine as this book goes to press), the fire that I felt years before to serve the Lord was and is still burning inside of me. I thank God for the good health He has given me. I still feel as strong as a teenager and am determined to continue using my strength to serve Him.

Someone prophesied to me that my latter days would be greater than my former days, and I believe that it will be so. I thank God that many of those who have attended our training sessions over the years are bearing fruit, and some of them have large churches and church organizations of their own.

Not too very long ago, two of our former trainees, Ajarn David and Adjarn Chetah, gathered some six hundred church leaders from all over the country. I myself had a burning desire to visit all of the trainees and invite them to gather for a reunion to celebrate the 40th Anniversary of the founding of Christ to Thailand Mission. I can now report that God blessed this effort. Our 40th Anniversary celebration, held in Khonkaen under the leadership of our director, Rev. Sonny Legardo, was a success and was attended by around two hundred former trainees and pastors.

Brother Luciano and his wife came all the way from the United States to attend the celebration. What a good time we all had reminiscing about all the good things the Lord has done in our lives for the past forty years.

Then, after more than forty years in Thailand, I suddenly felt drawn back to my roots in the

Moving On?

Philippines. I fully believe that it is now time for me to serve God in the land of my birth. I want to have a training center there which will be a copy of our training center here in Thailand.

We will have a short-term classroom training of three months and then a field training of eight months before a student can graduate. The trainees will be sent to every province to plant churches, and they will support their ministry by finding work in their places of ministry.

God willing, this training will spread to the neighboring countries of Burma, Malaysia, Indonesia, Singapore and others. This is my plan, but I will not do anything outside of the will of God. If this plan is God's will, then He will provide a way for it to happen. If not, then whatever, whenever and wherever, let God's will be done.

Amen!

Author Contact Page

You may contact Pedro Belardo in the following ways:

https://jmbelardo.wixsite.com/
livingoutthegospel

pedrojr707@gmail.com

Above: With my children and grandson
Below: With my daughter Joy

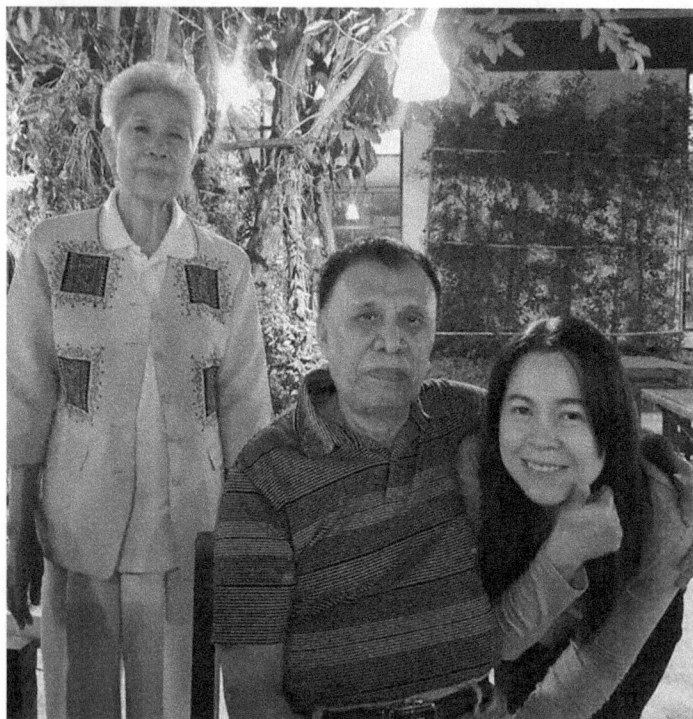

With my daughter-in-law and her mother.

www.ingramcontent.com/pod-product-compliance
Lightning Source LLC
Chambersburg PA
CBHW031604040426
42452CB00006B/399